Welcome to the World
A JEWISH BABY'S RECORD BOOK

ILLUSTRATOR
Glenn Wolff

ART DIRECTOR
Carol Isaak

WOMEN'S LEAGUE FOR CONSERVATIVE JUDAISM

שלשה שותפים באדם:

הקב"ה אביו ואמו.

נדה ל"א

First edition December 1985
Second printing 1988
Third printing 1991
Fourth Edition November 1996
ISBN # 0-936293-00-4

© 1985 Women's League for Conservative Judaism
    48 East 74 Street
    New York, NY 10021

Three are partners in the molding
of every human being:
God, the father and the mother

Talmud, Nidah:31

This book is dedicated to

_____

Child's Name

Hospital Memorabilia

Affix an envelope to the inside cover and enclose:

☐ Baby's footprints   ☐ Fingerprints   ☐ Hospital bracelet   ☐ Newborn photograph   *(check box if included)*

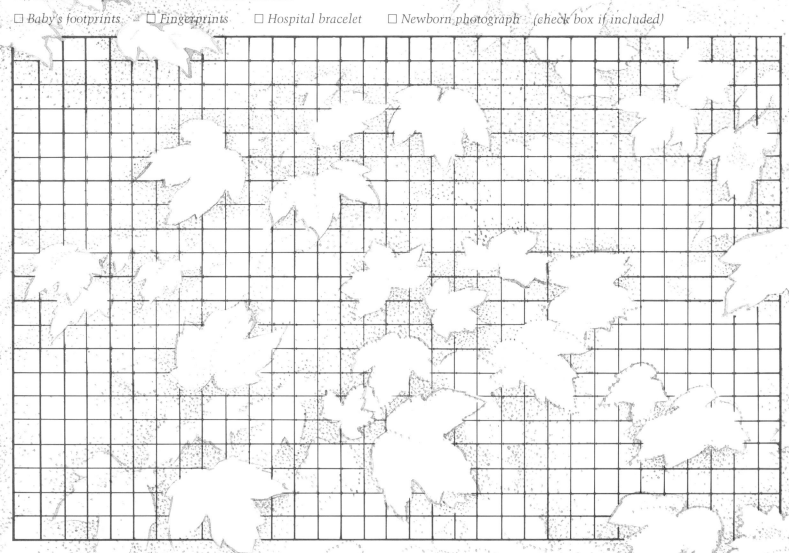

Vital Statistics

Born on _____ month _____ date _____ year _____
　　　　　day of the week

corresponding on Hebrew calendar to the _____ day of _____ 57 _____
　　　　　　　　　　　　　　　　　　　　　　　　　　　　　　　　month　　　　　　　*year*

at _____ o'clock　a.m.　p.m.

Place _____ Sedrah of the Week _____

Delivered by _____ Nurse _____

Others present _____ Pediatrician _____

Method of delivery _____

Physical Characteristics

Color of eyes at birth _____ Color of eyes later _____

Color of hair _____ eyebrows _____ eyelashes _____

Shape of head _____ Circumference _____

Weight _____ Length _____ Apgar Score _____

Blood type _____ Identification Marks _____

Looks just like _____

Birth registered at _____ Certificate number _____

Our Feelings...Reactions...Impressions

MOTHER'S PAGE / Prenatal and the Birth Experience

ישמח האב ביוצא חלציו The father will rejoice in the
ותגל האם בפרי בטנה outpouring of his loins, and
ככתוב: ישמח אביך ואמך the mother will delight in
ותגל יולדתך. the fruit of her womb.

FATHER'S PAGE / Prenatal and the Birth Experience

A Good Name

טוב שם משמן טוב   A good name is better than precious oil

Kohelet 7.1

Child's English Name

Child's Hebrew Name

Why the names were chosen

Coming Home

ברוך אתה יי We praise You, Lord our God, King
אלהינו מלך העולם, of the Universe, Who has kept us in
שהחינו וקימנו והגיענו life, sustained us and enabled us to
לזמן הזה. reach this occasion

Date _____ Time _____

Transportation _____ Weather _____

Address _____

Accompanied by _____

Welcomed by _____

Baby's "Own Corner" _____

_____

_____

_____

Who said what: _____

_____

_____

_____

_____

_____

_____

Naming a Daughter

Traditionally, a daughter is named in the Synagogue on an occasion when the Torah is being read. Her father (or both parents) or an appropriate surrogate is given an **Aliyah**; a special blessing **Mi Shebayrakh** is recited and the name is announced.

Following the ceremony, a **Se'udat Mitzvah** (festive meal), whether in the Synagogue or at home, is appropriate at this joyous milestone. Increasingly popular are a wide variety of meaningful and creative home ceremonies.

Birkat Hagomayl — Blessing of Thanks
After the birth of a child (whether a son or a daughter), it is appropriate for the mother to visit the Synagogue when the Torah is read, to say the prayer of thanks designated for recitation after being delivered from danger or after recovery from a grave illness.

בָּרוּךְ אַתָּה יְיָ אֱלֹהֵינוּ מֶלֶךְ הָעוֹלָם, הַגּוֹמֵל לְחַיָבִים טוֹבוֹת, שֶׁגְּמָלַנִי כָּל טוֹב.

Praised are You, Lord our God, King of the Universe, Who has graciously bestowed His great goodness upon me.

Comments _____

_____

_____

_____

_____

_____

_____

_____

שמחת בת

מי שברך אבותינו May He Who blessed our ancestors, Abraham, Isaac and Jacob, Sarah,
אברהם יצחק ויעקב Rebecca, Rachel and Leah, bless these parents:
שרה רבקה רחל ולאה
הוא יברך את־ההורים

_____ and _____
Father's English Name   *Mother's English Name*

ואת בתם הנולדה להם and their newborn child. May her name be called in Israel
ויקרא שמה בישראל

_____ ו _____ בת _____
Mother's Hebrew Name   *Father's Hebrew Name*   *Child's Hebrew Name*

_____
Child's Complete English Name

יהי רצון שיזכו הוריה May the parents rear their daughter to maturity imbued with
לגדלה לתורה ולחפה the love of Torah and the fulfillment of mitzvot, and may they
ולמעשים טובים. be privileged to bring her to the wedding canopy.

_____ _____
Date   *Officiant*

_____
Place

The Covenant of Circumcision

"Praised are You, O Lord our God, King of the Universe, Who sanctified us with Your commandments, and commanded us to bring our son into the covenant of Abraham, our father."

בָּרוּךְ אַתָּה יְיָ אֱלֹהֵינוּ מֶלֶךְ הָעוֹלָם, אֲשֶׁר קִדְּשָׁנוּ בְּמִצְוֹתָיו, וְצִוָּנוּ לְהַכְנִיסוֹ בִּבְרִיתוֹ שֶׁל אַבְרָהָם אָבִינוּ.

Brit Milah, the oldest continuing Jewish ritual, is one of three major covenants recorded in the Torah. The first is Shabbat, the setting aside of time as a symbol of creation; the second is the rainbow, a phenomenon of nature testifying to God's promise to Noah following the flood; the third, the **brit** (convenant) of circumcision, is the physical sign which marks the initiation of the child into the people of Israel.

Brit Milah should be performed on the eighth day, by a **mohel,** who is trained in both the **halakhah** and the surgical procedure. The **berakhah** is recited by the father or an appropriate surrogate.

Honored participants in the ceremony are the **Sandek** who holds the child during the procedure, and the **Kvater** and **Kvaterin** (godfather and godmother) who bring the baby to the **Sandek.**

Other individuals may be invited to lead **Hamotzi** and **Birkat Hamazon** at the **Se'udat Mitzvah** (festive meal) which traditionally follows the ceremony.

Comments _____

_____

_____

_____

_____

_____

_____

ברית מילה

מי שברך אבותינו May He Who blessed our ancestors, Abraham, Isaac and Jacob, Sarah,
אברהם יצחק ויעקב Rebecca, Rachel and Leah, bless these parents:
שרה רבקה רחל ולאה
הוא יברך את־ההורים

_____ and _____
Father's English Name   *Mother's English Name*

ואת בנם הנולד להם and their newborn child. May his name be called in Israel:
ויקרא שמו בישראל

_____ ו _____ בן _____
Mother's Hebrew Name   *Father's Hebrew Name*   *Child's Hebrew Name*

_____
Child's Complete English Name

יהי רצון שיזכו הוריו May the parents rear their son to maturity imbued with
לגדלו לתורה ולחפה the love of Torah and the fulfillment of mitzvot, and may they
ולמעשים טובים. be privileged to bring him to the wedding canopy.

_____   _____
Mohel/Officiant   *Rabbi*

_____   _____   _____
Sandek   *Kvater*   *Kvaterin*

_____   _____
Date   *Place*

Family Tree

דור לדר

Generation to Generation

Pidyon Haben

פדיון הבן

In accordance with the Biblical injunction, "sanctify unto Me the first born", the first born son of every Israelite family in ancient times was vested with special responsibilities in assisting the **Kohanim** in the conduct of worship. With the construction of the Tabernacle, this vocation of the first-born was transferred to the tribe of **Levi.** The Torah then decreed the redemption from service of every first-born son not of the tribe of **Levi,** by payment of five **shekalim** to a **Kohen.**

On the 31st day after the birth of a first-born son, the ceremony of redemption is enacted.* A **Kohen**, tracing his descent from the ancient tribe, is invited to participate. In the presence of a **minyan,** a dialogue ensues between the father and the **Kohen.** After accepting five **shekalim,**

the **Kohen** returns the child to his father and blesses the child with the threefold priestly benediction.

May the Lord bless you and guard you. May the Lord show you favor and be gracious unto you. May the Lord show you kindness and grant you peace.

יְבָרֶכְךָ יְיָ וְיִשְׁמְרֶךָ.

יָאֵר יְיָ פָּנָיו אֵלֶיךָ וִיחֻנֶּךָ.

יִשָּׂא יְיָ פָּנָיו אֵלֶיךָ וְיָשֵׂם לְךָ שָׁלוֹם.

A festive meal (**Se'udat Mitzvah**) follows.

*If either maternal or paternal grandfather is a **Kohen** or **Levi** the grandson is exempt from **Pidyon Haben**, as is a first born son delivered by Caesarian section.*

Date

Place

Name of Kohen

Coinage Used

Gifts

Gift	from	Gift	from

When Baby Arrived......

SPECIAL HEADLINES

Local News

World News

In Israel

In the Sports World

IN THE CULTURAL WORLD

Books _____

_____

_____

Movies _____

_____

Theatre _____

_____

Radio & TV _____

_____

_____

Music _____

_____

_____

Fashion _____

_____

Growth & Immunization Chart

	Weight	Length/Height
Date — First Doctor's Visit		
1 Month		
2 Months		
3 Months		
4 Months		
5 Months		
6 Months		
8 Months		
1 Year		
18 Months		
2 Years		
30 Months		
3 Years		

Date/First DPT	Date/Second Polio	Date/TB (Tine) Test	Date/Mumps
Date/First Polio	Date/Third DPT	Date/Measles	Date/Fourth Polio
Date/Second DPT	Date/Third Polio	Date/Rubella	Date/Other

Visits to Doctor & Dentist

Date

Doctor

Reason & Doctor's Comments

Date/First Tooth

Teething Problems

Date/Lost First Tooth

Date/First Permanent Tooth

Date

Dentist

Reason

Baby's Intellectual Development

Responds to voice

Date   Describe

First social smile

Recognizes mother or other
frequently seen person

Reaches out to other
children

Calls adults for help

Plays with own feet

Plays peek-a-boo

Reaches and pats
mirror image

Fears strangers

Prefers one hand to
another (which hand)

Looks at picture book
with interest

Builds tower of two-three
blocks after demonstration

Responds to own name

Comments

Physical Development

The sequence of a child's development will not always occur in this order.

	Date		Date
Moves head from side to side	_____	Sidesteps along furniture; cruises	_____
Holds head up	_____	Can sit down from standing position	_____
Rolls from front to back	_____	Walks holding two hands	_____
Rolls from back to front	_____	Stands unsupported	_____
Reaches for objects	_____	Sleeps through the night	_____
Discovers hands	_____	Steps out alone	_____
Fingers, hands in mutual play	_____	Climbs out of crib	_____
Transfers a toy from one hand to another	_____	Moves to rhythm	_____
Accomplishes a grasp	_____	Tries to sing	_____
Plays with rattle	_____	Pedals small tricycle	_____
Sits supported	_____	Swims	_____
Sits unsupported	_____	Toilet trained day	_____
Pulls self to sit	_____	Toilet trained night	_____
Crawls	_____	Sleeps in a bed	_____
Pushes up on hands and knees and rocks	_____		
Stands alone when pulled up	_____		
Pulls self to stand	_____		

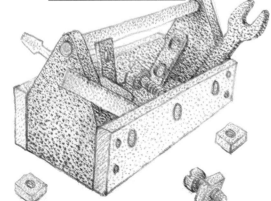

Hearty Appetite

Nursed

_____
Date

Weaned from breast

_____

Formula type

_____

Weaned from bottle

_____

First solid food

_____

Reaction to solids

_____

Begins finger food

_____
Date

Holds own bottle

_____

Drinks from a cup

_____

Plays with utensils

_____

Feeds self entire meal

_____

Comments _____

_____

_____

_____

_____

_____

_____

_____

Baby's Shabbat Experiences

Baby's Holiday Experiences

Rosh Hashanah
and Yom Kippur _____

_____

_____

_____

_____

Sukkot _____

_____

_____

Simḥat Torah _____

_____

_____

Hanukkah _____

_____

_____

_____

_____

_____

Tu BiShevat _____

_____

Purim _____

_____

_____

_____

_____

Pesah _____

_____

_____

_____

Lag Ba'Omer _____

_____

_____

Shavu'ot _____

_____

_____

Yom Ha'Atzma'ut _____

_____

Baby's "Firsts"

Play Group

_____
Where & date

_____
With whom

Nursery School

_____
Where & date

_____
With whom

Kindergarten

_____
Where & date

_____
With whom

Visit to the Synagogue

_____ | _____
Where & date | *With whom*

First Prayer

_____ | _____
Where & date | *With whom*

Plane Ride

_____ | _____
Where & date | *With whom*

Bus Ride

_____ | _____
Where & date | *With whom*

Boat Ride

_____ | _____
Where & date | *With whom*

Train Ride

_____ | _____
Where & date | *With whom*

Haircut

_____ | _____
Where & date | *With whom*

Baby Celebrates

Birthdays _____

_____

_____

_____

_____

_____

Secular holidays and family occasions _____

_____

_____

_____

_____

_____

_____

Baby's Adventures

At Home

In the Neighborhood

In the Big World _____

Baby's Favorite Things

Toys _____

_____

Games _____

_____

Books _____

_____

Songs _____

_____

TV Programs _____

_____

Pets _____

_____

"Security" Object _____

_____

Other Activities _____

_____

Baby's Favorite People

Quotables

LANGUAGE DEVELOPMENT

Makes sounds

Date _____

Mama _____

Dada

Two syllable utterances
(choo-choo) _____

Begins to recognize
words _____

Shouts for attention _____

Says "no" _____

Says "bye bye" _____

First ten words

1. _____   6. _____

2. _____   7. _____

3. _____   8. _____

4. _____   9. _____

5. _____   10. _____

Especially appropriate
"invented" words _____

_____

First Hebrew words _____

_____

Tales to tell _____

_____

_____

_____

_____

_____

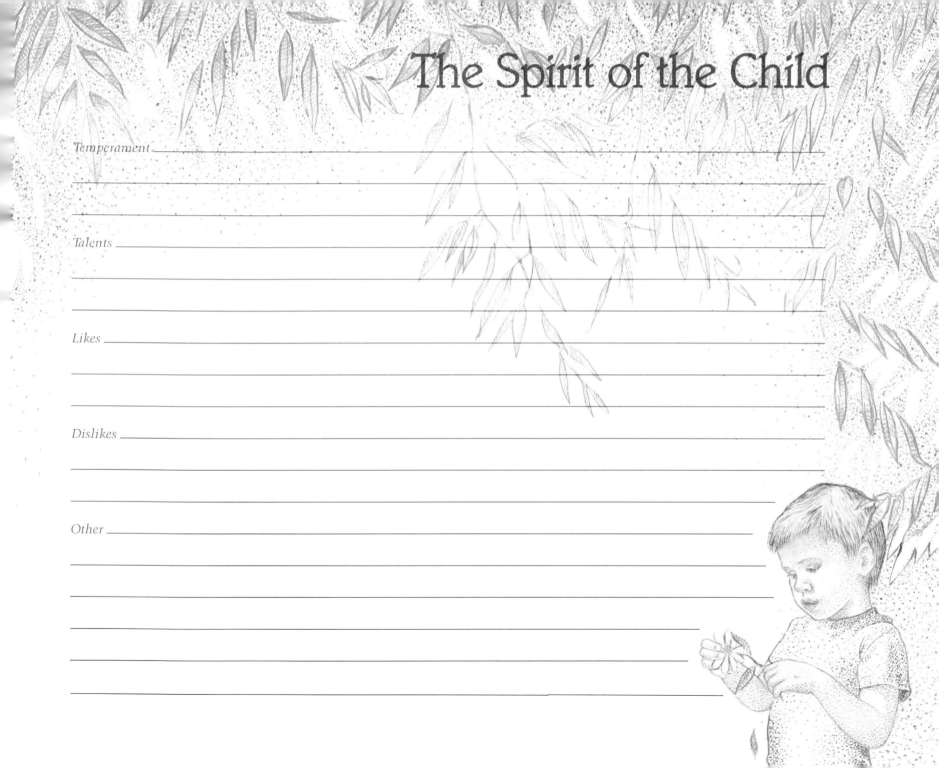

The Spirit of the Child

Temperament _____

_____

_____

Talents _____

_____

Likes _____

_____

_____

Dislikes _____

_____

_____

Other _____

_____

_____

_____

_____

...And We'll Always Remember...

Childhood is a crown of roses   Talmud, Shabbat

Favorite Activities in Pictures

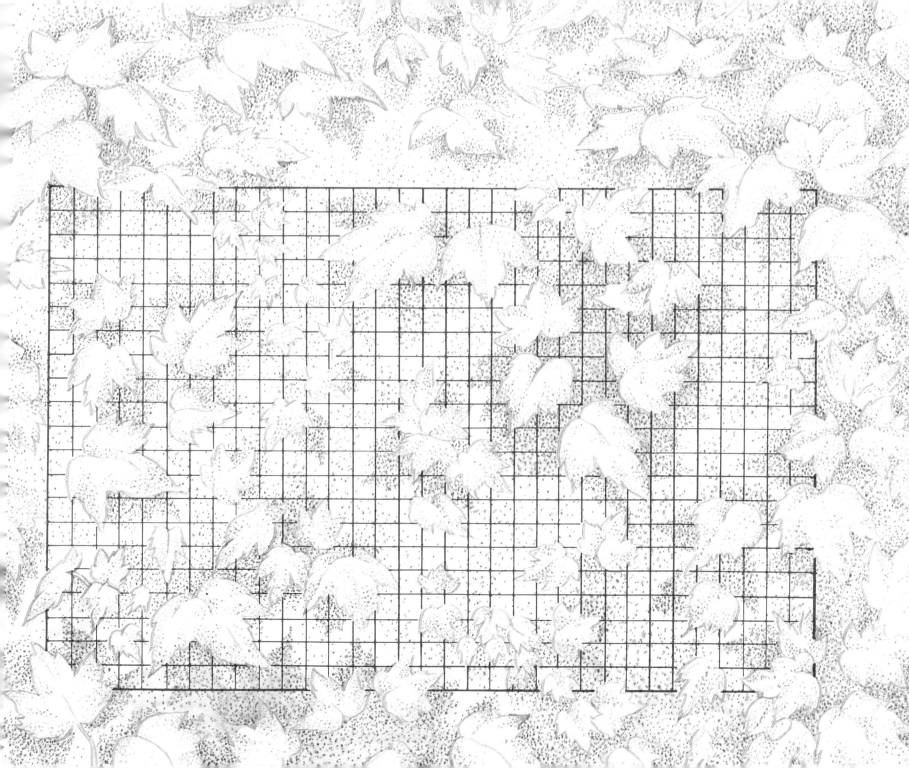

God's Time

Living is not a private affair of the individual.
Living is what man does with God's time,
What man does with God's world.

Abraham Joshua Heschel

Comments _____

_____

_____

_____

_____

_____

_____

_____

_____

_____

_____

_____